Lunch at t

Wendy Blaxlan
illustrated by Christina Brimage

ISBN 0-590-23789-6

12 11 10 9/9 0 1 2/0

Printed in the U.S.A. 08

First Scholastic printing, January 1997

SCHOLASTIC INC.
New York Toronto London Auckland Sydney

‘This is *my* lunch,’ said the elephant.
‘Yum! Yum!’

‘This is *my* lunch,’ said the lion.
‘Yum! Yum!’

'This is *my* lunch,' said the seal.
'Yum! Yum!'

'This is *my* lunch,' said the monkey.
'Yum! Yum!'

'This is *my* lunch,' said the panda.
'Yum! Yum!'

‘This is *my* lunch,’ said the zoo keeper.
‘Yum! Yum!’

‘This is *my* lunch,’ said the seagull.
‘Yum! Yum!’